Downers Grove Public Library
1050 Curtiss
Downers Grove, Il. 60515

DEMCO

8/09-69x

TIGER SHARKS

Anne Welsbacher

Capstone Press

MINNEAPOLIS

Capstone Press • 2440 Fernbrook Lane • Minneapolis, MN 55447

Editorial Director   John Coughlan
Managing Editor   John Martin
Production Editor   James Stapleton
Copy Editor   Thomas Streissguth

*Photo Credits: ©Doug Perrine/Innerspace Visions-Miami,
FL: pp. 6, 8-9, 11, 12, 20, 26, 28, 29, 32, 33, 40, 41; ©Ron
and Valerie Taylor/Innerspace Visions-Miami, FL: 15, 16,
30, 39; ©Jeff Rotman: pp. 22, 25, 36; ©James D.
Watt/Innerspace Visions-Miami, FL: pp. 19. 42-43.*

Library of Congress Cataloging-in-Publication Data
Welsbacher, Anne, 1955-
  Tiger sharks / by Anne Welsbacher.
   p. cm. -- (Sharks)
  Includes bibliographical references and index.
  ISBN 1-56065-269-1
  1. Tiger shark--Juvenile literature. [1. Tiger shark.
  2. Sharks.] I. Title. II. Series: Welsbacher, Anne, 1955-
  Sharks.
  QL638.95.C3W45 1996
  597'.31--dc20   95-7867
                                                    CIP
                                                    AC
99 98 97 96 95   6 5 4 3 2 1

Table of Contents

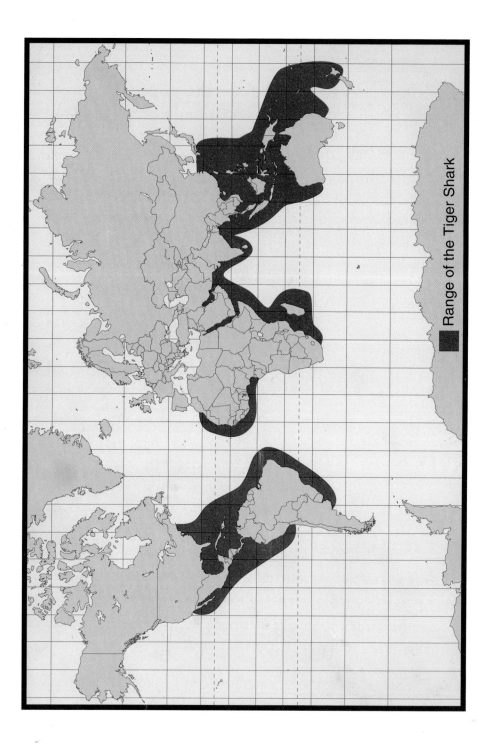

Range of the Tiger Shark

Facts about Tiger Sharks

Scientific name: *Galeocerdo cuvier*

Closest relatives: The tiger shark is the only member of its genus (Galeocerdo); other members of its family include the blue shark, lemon shark, and gray shark.

Description: A big broad shark with a short snout that looks square from above and pointed from the side. The upper part of the tail is pointed and is at least three times longer than the bottom part.

Length: Tiger sharks average 10 to 14 feet (3 to 4 meters) long, with females slightly larger than males. They may reach 23 feet (7 meters).

Weight: An average tiger shark weighs 1600 pounds (700 kilograms). Some weigh more than 3 tons (1,500 kilograms).

Color: Gray. Adults have darker gray stripes on their backs.

Food: Fish and squid.

Location: Tiger sharks swim in the warm and temperate (nearly warm) ocean waters near land.

Chapter 1
Swimming Trash Cans

They're sometimes called swimming trash cans. And for good reason–tiger sharks will eat anything.

You could fill a house with the things that have been found in tiger sharks' stomachs. Nuts and bolts, boat cushions, tin cans, and driftwood. Wallets, shoes, straw hats, and trousers. Alarm clocks and tom-toms. Bricks, bottles, and beer cans. Watches and license plates. Overcoats, belts, and shoes. A tree trunk. One tiger shark even ate a chicken coop, with feathers and bones still inside it.

Alive or Dead

Tiger sharks are among the fiercest **predators** in the sea. The stomachs of tiger sharks have been found to contain rats and dogs, sheep and turtles, a crocodile's head, lobsters, and conch.

Tiger sharks often eat other sharks. One tiger shark had a bull shark inside it. Inside the bull shark there was a black-tip shark. And inside the black-tip was a dogfish shark! The man who caught the tiger could claim a record for the most fish on one hook.

Fortunately, most sharks don't eat again for days, or even weeks, after a big meal.

One of the Three Most Dangerous

The tiger shark was named for the way it looks. Like the big cat, the adult tiger shark has stripes on its back.

It has an attitude a lot like a tiger's, too. It is a swift and powerful killer. Its Latin name, *Galeocerdo,* means "cunning."

A scientist jabs an identification tag into a big tiger shark. These tags allow scientists to follow the shark's movements.

The tiger shark is the second largest of the three most dangerous sharks in the sea. These are the great white shark, the tiger shark, and the bull shark. The tiger shark is second only to the great white shark in the number of recorded attacks on swimmers.

11

The wedge-shaped head of a tiger shark allows it to make quick turns in the water.

The Tiger Shark's Body

The tiger shark has a big, broad head that looks almost square from above. Instead of a sharp, pointed snout, the front of its head is shaped like a wide wedge. Its nostrils are clearly visible on the corners of its square snout. Its body, and especially its head, are shaped for making quick turns in the water.

These sharks are dark gray-brown or bluish-green, almost black, on the top, or dorsal, side and white or light yellow on the bottom, or **ventral**, side. Their spots and stripes are light shades of the main dark color.

On the shark's side are five slits in the skin. These are called **gill slits**. A tiger shark's gill slits are not as big as some sharks', but they do the job of letting out water.

How do they work? The shark takes in water through its mouth. The water passes over the gills, which remove oxygen from it. Then the water leaves the body through the gill slits.

Tiger sharks also have tiny gill slits located behind their eyes. They provide oxygen that goes right to the eyes and brain through a separate blood vessel.

The Tiger Shark's Size

This shark is one of the big ones. An average tiger shark may be 10 to 14 feet (3 to 4 meters) long. They have been known to reach as much as 23 feet (7 meters).There have even been reports of tiger sharks 30 feet (9 meters) long, but these probably are not true. They often weigh more than a ton (0.9 metric tons) and sometimes as much as three tons (2.7 metric tons).

Tigers have long, pointed tail fins. The upper part of the fin is much longer than the lower one.

There are hard ridges where the body narrows for the tail attachment. These ridges look like bone, but they are made up of **cartilage**. That's the tough tissue that humans have in their noses, ears, and kneecaps.

Where Tigers Live

Tiger sharks are loners except when mating. They swim in warm waters around the world, usually staying near the coasts of continents. In northern summer, when the sea warms up, they may head farther north. During the southern summer, their territory expands farther south.

A school of sharks roams off a surfing beach in Australia.

Like blue sharks and makos, tigers travel long distances, sometimes 50 miles (80 kilometers) or more in a day. During the evening and night, they swim into shallow, coastal waters to feed and rest. In the daytime, they swim out to the open seas.

Chapter 2
The Appetite of a Tiger Shark

Tiger sharks are slow cruisers–until they spot dinner. Then they speed up.

A tiger shark circles its prey for a long time before attacking. It watches the prey. It might bump it with its fins or snout.

Then it attacks — fast. It stiffens and hunches its back. It speeds toward the prey. As it approaches, it pulls its large **pectoral**, or side, fins down. This is like hitting the brakes on a car.

It lifts its head and uses special muscles to open its huge mouth wide. As in all sharks, the tiger sharks' upper jaws are not attached to the skull. When the shark is ready to bite, it can push its jaw forward to grab the food.

The shark stabs its prey with its lower teeth—like driving a fork into a steak. Then it uses the teeth in both jaws to saw off slabs of meat. It swings its body side to side for more slicing force.

Recognized by Its Teeth

Tigers have very wide and large mouths across their broad, flat heads. When the mouth is closed, no teeth show. But when it opens, it opens very wide, revealing pointed teeth.

The edges of the teeth are **serrated**, or edged like a saw. The outer side of each tooth has a deep notch in it, making it look like a bumpy triangle. A tiger can always be recognized by its odd-shaped teeth.

Like all sharks, tigers have rows of teeth behind the front teeth. When a front tooth breaks off, a new tooth moves into place. As the shark grows, new and bigger teeth move into place.

Tiger sharks have flat snouts and sharp, serrated teeth–ideal for slicing through the flesh of their prey.

Tigers have very strong jaws. Once they chomp into something, it's hard to pry them loose. They have been known to take a bite weighing 25 pounds (11 kilograms) or more out of the carcass of a whale.

This female tiger carries scars from the bites of a male during mating.

Eat Now, Digest Later

Tiger sharks sometimes eat now and digest later. If they swallow something they can't digest, they'll throw it up.

They can also store food to use later. When most large animals swallow food, the acids and other digestive fluids immediately start to act on the food. But there are no digestive fluids in a shark's stomach.

This stomach is like a holding cell, where food is stored until it can be digested later. This means that items found in tiger sharks' stomachs might still be in good shape.

The stomach of one tiger shark contained two dolphin fish four feet (1.2 meters) long. The dolphins were completely undigested.

The tiger shark's regular diet includes bony fish, smaller sharks, seals, dolphins, and stingrays. Because they have such strong, thick jaws and teeth, tiger sharks can also eat creatures with shells, like lobsters, crabs, and clams. Unlike most sharks, tigers eat sea snakes and sea turtles–shells and all.

Chapter 3
A Tiger Shark's Life

Like all sharks, tiger sharks depend on their senses to find food and survive.

Smelling

Scientists say that sharks can smell one part of blood in one million parts of water. And they can smell it from a quarter of a mile (about 400 meters) away. More of the shark's brain is used for smelling than for any other sense. Sharks are more likely to follow their noses than their eyes in hunting for food.

A Special Eyelid

Tiger sharks have a special protective eyelid–called the third eyelid or **nictitating membrane**–that can close over the eye, shielding it from fighting prey. The ferocious great white shark does not have a nictitating membrane. The eyelid is sometimes used to identify an attacking shark as a tiger shark.

Hearing by Touch

Besides hearing regular sounds, all sharks also "hear" by using a kind of "touch" sense. The **lateral line**, a strip of sensory cells along a shark's body and into its head and inner ear.

The lateral line picks up vibrations. All sound consists of vibrations, but the lateral line senses vibrations far too low for humans to hear. Sharks use the lateral line to "hear" thrashing fish and other distant motion.

The Sixth Sense

The shark's most unusual sense is a kind of "sixth sense" that no other animals have.

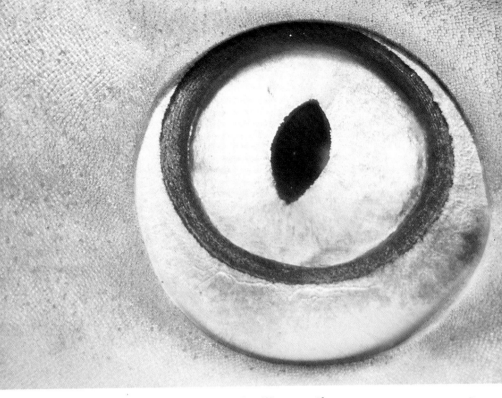

The eye of a lemon shark looks like a cat's eye.

Tiny pores around the shark's jaws are filled with fluid. These pores are called the **ampullae of Lorenzini**. Ampullae were small bottles in ancient Rome. The pores are shaped like these bottles. The man who discovered them was named Lorenzini.

All living creatures give off electrical signals, especially when their muscles are

Claspers and a lateral line can be seen on this sand tiger shark.

working. If a creature is wounded, the signals given off are even stronger. A shark's ampullae of Lorenzini sense these signals, and it swims toward them.

Plotting Escape

When a shark finds itself in a bad situation, it uses all its senses to study it. Valerie Taylor is a diver who has studied tiger and other sharks for many years. She once watched a tiger shark try to work its way out of a fenced area. The shark watched her come in every day. It watched the webbing that trapped it. It tried to work this webbing loose with its snout.

Taylor believes such behavior means that tiger sharks might be intelligent. Sharks might do much more "thinking" than we once believed. They might even "talk" to other sharks in ways we don't yet understand.

Mating and Giving Birth

Male tiger sharks, like all male sharks, use a modified fin called a **clasper** to mate with females. The pair of claspers, located on the bottom, or ventral, side, is used to hold onto the female. One clasper is inserted into an opening on the ventral side of the female. It acts as a channel to insert sperm into the female's body.

As a lemon shark gives birth, a remora appears neaby to feed on the mother's umbilical cord.

The fertilized eggs hatch inside the mother's body. The young continue to grow there. About nine months after mating, the mother gives birth to living young. These pups are 20 to 30 inches (50 to 75 centimeters) long at birth. The spotted pups are ready to swim and feed.

Tiger sharks usually give birth to up to 40 pups at a time. A female tiger shark caught off Cuba was 14 feet, 7 inches (4.3 meters) long. She carried within her 82 pups.

Tiger sharks grow slowly and are one of the longest-living sharks. They normally live 25 to 40 years. They may even get to be 50 years old.

The pup swims away after leaving the womb of its mother.

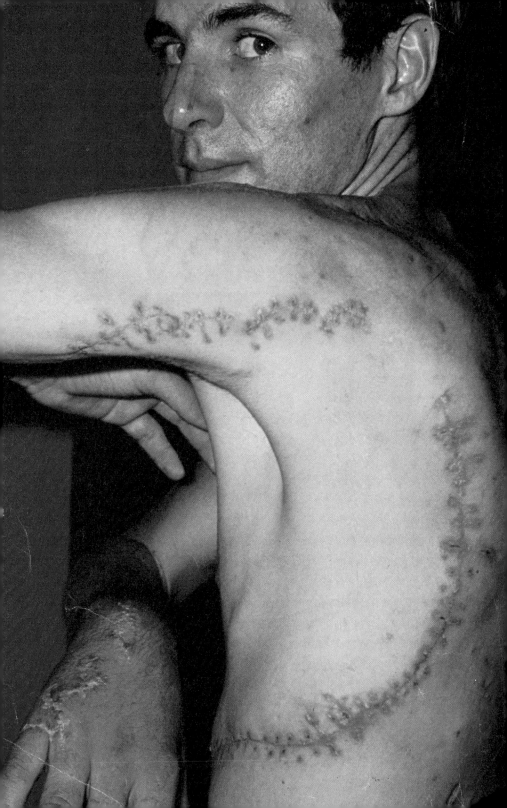

Chapter 4
The Shark Arm Murder and Other Mysteries

In 1935, a tiger shark was caught and moved to an aquarium in Australia. The shark would not eat for days. Then one day it vomited up things it had swallowed before being caught.

One of those things was a human arm. The arm had a tattoo on it. Experts could even make out the fingerprints of the hand.

The teeth of a great white shark made these scars in the back of Australian Rodney Fox.

The arm had been cut off by a knife, not bitten off by the shark. Because of the tattoo and fingerprints, officials knew the arm's owner was James Smith. A known thief, Smith had been reported missing. Officials believed that he had been involved in a crime and something had gone wrong. They thought he had been murdered and his body sawn to pieces.

A diver keeps his distance from a dangerous tiger shark.

A 12-foot tiger shark hunts for prey in the shallow waters off the Bahama Islands.

His body was never found. The court ruled that a body was needed to have a murder. One arm from a shark's stomach was not enough evidence to say that a murder had been committed.

The Shark Papers

In 1799, a United States ship called the *Nancy* was sailing to Haiti with goods to sell. The British were blockading Haiti to keep United States ships from doing business there.

A British ship captured the *Nancy*. But before officers could come aboard, the *Nancy*'s captain dumped all the ship's legal papers overboard. These papers showed that the ship was American. The captain replaced them with fake papers saying the ship was Dutch.

The British captain suspected foul play. He wanted to prove the ship was a United States ship. Then he could capture it. But he didn't have any way to prove it. It looked as if the *Nancy*'s captain would win his gamble.

But a hungry tiger shark and bad luck undid him.

A Big Breakfast

The day after the *Nancy* was captured, the captain of another ship was fishing nearby. He hooked a huge tiger shark.

He invited the British captain to his ship for breakfast. At the same time, his men opened up the tiger shark he had hooked.

Inside the shark were the papers thrown over board from the *Nancy*! Every word of the papers could still be read. It was proof that the *Nancy* was an American ship. The British captain took the *Nancy* as a lawful prize of war.

The Shark Papers, as they are called, are on display in Jamaica. The jaws of the tiger shark were displayed in London for a while. But they have since been lost.

Chapter 5
Shark Attack!

It was a cold Saturday in Australia in 1967. Two divers were practising for a spearfishing competition. They found a spot and began looking for fish to spear.

Suddenly a huge shark came from nowhere. It passed right under one of the divers. Then it grabbed the other diver. It bit him in half. The first diver saw the upper body of his friend float to the surface.

The shark turned to him. The shark's jaw was at least 2.5 feet (76 centimeters) wide. The diver could see his friend's feet, still hanging

A diver pulls on an anti-shark suit before braving shark-infested waters.

out of the shark's mouth. He stabbed at the shark's eye with his spear. The protective third eyelid quickly covered it.

The shark was circling. It didn't attack the diver, and it didn't feed on the dead man.

As fast as he could, the frightened diver swam the 750 yards (700 meters) back to the beach.

Because of its size and the special third eyelid over its eyes, officials were certain it was a tiger shark. The diver who survived never knew why the tiger shark passed him by and killed his friend instead.

The Shark Attack File

In 1958, a group of scientists created the Shark Attack File. In the Shark Attack File they put reports and photographs of all known shark attacks.

Tiger sharks swim too close for comfort to many Australian beaches.

Of the more than 370 types of sharks, only about 30 have attacked humans. Three types account for most attacks. These are the great white shark, the tiger shark, and the bull shark.

Other sharks considered dangerous are the hammerheads, shortfin makos, nurse sharks, gray reef sharks, and lemon sharks.

The tiger shark accounts for several attacks on humans.

Many fishermen consider the tiger shark a good game fish. This species will put up a good fight—but they're also dangerous out of the water.

Tiger Shark Attacks

There have been 27 reports of attacks on humans by tiger sharks. They are the most dangerous sharks in warm, tropical waters. Florida and Hawaii have had many tiger shark attacks.

In an Australian attack in 1937, two men were killed by one shark. Parts of each of them were found the next day in the stomach of a 850-pound (386-kilogram) tiger shark.

Oddly, tiger sharks don't always seem to like people. Scuba divers have reported tiger sharks swimming right past them, ignoring them completely.

Mistaken Identity

When tiger sharks do attack people, it may be by mistake. A person on a surfboard, seen from below, could look a lot like a seal. People kicking and splashing on the water's surface also make the same noises as fish swimming in sharks' waters.

The tiger shark sometimes attacks boats. But the sharks may not actually be attacking the boat. Instead, they may be going after a fish flopping on a fishing line. They might even be going after a moving oar, thinking it is a fish. The boat just happens to be in the way.

People Attacking the Tiger Shark

Tiger sharks attack boats, and people in boats attack tiger sharks. Many people think tiger sharks are good game fish because they put up a big fight. Some other sharks, like Greenland sharks, are easy to catch. But the tiger shark fights with great thrashing.

The largest tiger shark ever caught was hooked off South Carolina in 1964. Its weight was 1,780 pounds (811.7 kilograms).

Glossary

ampullae of Lorenzini–fluid-filled sacs in sharks that can sense vibrations and help sharks "hear"

cartilage–a stiff but bendable body tissue. Sharks have a skeleton made of cartilage instead of bone.

claspers–a pair of organs located on the abdomen on a male shark, used for mating. They look like extra fins.

dorsal–located on the back

gill slits–the long straight openings on the side of a shark into which water flows. A tiger shark has five gill slits.

lateral line–a row of special sensory cells that lies along the side of a shark. It senses motion in the water.

nictitating membrane–an extra eyelid, which can close to protect the eye. It is also called the third eyelid.

pectoral–located on the sides

predator–an animal that hunts for and eats other animals

serrated–saw-toothed

ventral–located on the stomach side

To Learn More

Blassingame, Wyatt. *Wonders of Sharks.* New York: Dodd, Mead, and Co., 1984.

Cerullo, Mary M. *Sharks: Challengers of the Deep.* New York: Cobblehill Books, 1993.

Freedman, Russel. *Sharks.* New York: Holiday House, 1985.

Langley, Andrew. *The World of Sharks.* New York: Bookwright Press, 1987.

Springer Victor G. and Joy P. Gould. *Sharks In Question: The Smithsonian Answer Book.* 1989.

Steel, Rodney. *Sharks of the World.* New York: Facts on File, 1989.

Sharks, Silent Hunters of the Deep, Readers Digest, 1987.

Index